The Daycare Bible

A Comprehensive Guide to Choosing a Daycare For Your Child, Birth to Age 3

Khadija Anderson

Copyright © 2016 by Khadija Anderson

All rights reserved. No part of this publication may be reproduced, distributed, or transmitted in any form or by any means, including photocopying, recording, or other electronic or mechanical means, or stored in a database or retrieval system, without the prior written permission of the author, except in the case of brief quotations embodied in critical reviews and other non-commercial uses permitted by copyright law.

For permission requests, please email the author, subject line: "The Daycare Bible Permissions" at littlebohemiansdaycare@gmail.com

Identifying details, including names, have been withheld except by permission.

Special thanks and endless love to all my families, and especially my very own: Seamus, Mariama, Amina, Remi, and Flynn.

Cover Photo: Khadija Anderson with permission

Contents

Preface 5

I. Basics 7

Why did I write this book? 8
Choices, choices, choices 12
Licensed or not, what's the big deal? 13
What is a small progressive daycare? 18
More-Kids-Versus-Less-Kids in a nutshell 19

2. Nuts & Bolts 21

Philosophies and Caregiving Styles 22
Play Based Learning vs. Activities or Curriculum 25
Outdoor, Indoor, & Infant Play Environments 27
Why are all these toddlers with my infant? 32
Transitioning new children 36

3. One Day at a Time 39

Supplies: Diapers, wipes, clothing, shoes, chemicals 40
Food, choking, and the importance of water 43
Illness 47
Naps and sleeping 52
Potty Readiness 54
Communication with Your Caregiver 57
In The Land of No: Solving common toddler issues 59

Communication with Young Children	65
Bullies, biters and bad toddlers	66

4. Last But Not Least 71

Gender Neutrality or Boys will be boys (or will they?)	72
Anti-Bias, Multicultural Education	76
Creating Community	78
What to Ask a Potential Caregiver	80

Bibliography 83

Preface

This book deals specifically with daycare designed for infants, toddlers (including two year olds); birth to age 3. Infants and toddlers express themselves differently in an environment that is overflowing with children than they do in an environment that has very few children with whom they can create familial social bonds. Also, adults involved (be they caregivers or parents) have a different interaction together within that small group. This book is based on and dedicated to providing parents information leading them away from the large center model and specifically towards finding care with a provider who cares for a small group of four to five infants and/or toddlers.

In writing this book I have purposely chosen to be gender neutral by not disclosing or assigning gender to the children exampled. I have also chosen to use the term "parents" throughout to represent any adults be they biological or adoptive parent/s, guardians, caring relatives, or any other marvelous combination of adults who are integral to a child's life.

I. Basics

Why did I write this book?

The path to owning my own small daycare was long and winding. When my middle daughter was three years old, I discovered a beautiful Montessori school that did not prescribe what the child must do, but actually practiced Maria Montessori's dictum "Follow the Child". True to Montessori theory, it was a place where if a child wasn't using the materials the way in which they were shown, or were uninterested and perhaps lying in the middle of the floor, as long as they weren't being destructive they wouldn't be redirected to another activity (unfortunately, redirection is a common occurrence in many Montessori schools). The children were allowed to meet their own developmental needs within the rich environment of the classroom, which had been prepared to allow for that very thing.

I decided I wanted to work in that world and over the course of several years tried to get my (expensive) Montessori Teachers Certificate. Unfortunately, as a struggling single mother, I was never able to fully complete my training, but my studies allowed me to have jobs in several wonderful schools as an assistant teacher. After working in classrooms for about 5 years, I went back to college to get my BA and was able to revisit Dr. Montessori's philosophy while studying alternative Early Childhood Education pedagogies. Being in the classroom and then going back and revisiting the materials was very enlightening for me. I was able to fully grasp what it was that Montessori had discovered and why "follow the child" was an important thing to do.

After working from 1999 to 2005 with preschoolers and toddlers in a variety of settings including small and large centers and schools, and my own in-home Montessori preschool, I had the unfortunate experience of two nightmare jobs back to back (both of these centers closed within a year of my quitting). When I quit the last one I was quite traumatized and decided to try something else.

In looking through job listings in the Early Childhood Education/Daycare field I kept noticing ads for "Nanny Share". A Nanny Share is an arrangement whereby two families share one nanny and split the cost. This was a new concept to me and I thought I would try it. Since I was worried about caregiving in someone else's home where I would have no control over childproofing and supplies, I decided to run an ad on Craigslist offering a Nanny Share in my home for a few dollars less than the going rate.

I immediately got several families who were interested. Even though I was charging more than a daycare, I was still less than a Nanny Share and way less than a private Nanny. I began by caring for two children along with my youngest daughter who was two at the time. A year later, I moved to a larger space and expanded to one part-time and two full-time children since my daughter was now in preschool half-day.

The following year found me relocating to Los Angeles, where I once again relied on Craigslist to bring me families. I was now in a much larger house and could accommodate more children. Licensing let me have six, but there was something very appealing to working with a small group and so I kept my maximum to four children at a time. Four children was and still is the magic number for me.

For the first three or four years working with a small group I thought I had just mis-read my Early Childhood Education books which said that young children do not socialize but rather engage in what is called side-by-side play. They do indeed play side by side. One child will go to the sandbox and soon they are all there. One will go over and grab a ball and soon it is a ball fest. It is for this reason that I always try to have four of each toy, but more on that later. What I discovered was that young children under the age of three don't behave in the same manner in a small group as they do in a large group.

One day, as I was watching the children play, which included moments such as the children taking another's water bottle and not drinking from it but handing it to the other child, "sharing" toys, calling each other by name (for those that can talk), or sharing hugs or laughs, it dawned on me that what was occurring wasn't just a fluke, but the norm. Those Early Childhood Education books were written for caregivers expected to work in a much larger setting with a much larger group of children. What I was consistently witnessing was socialization. Just what the books said couldn't happen with this age group was indeed happening. And the reason why, which dawned on me that day, was that this small group of children was not just in daycare together; they were a family. The small group setting allowed them to interact on a level that I had previously only observed on rare occasions in larger settings. I knew this was the magic ingredient. If infants and toddlers must be in a daycare situation, this is a more ideal atmosphere for the children to experience.

This is the reason for this book, while I will discuss many areas that will technically overlap with large centers, I hope to encourage families to find a small home based daycare that can provide their child with a unique, enriching, and positive experience.

Choices, choices, choices

In most communities, daycare choices include: a person who cares for one child and possibly also their own child in their home, a nanny or nanny share (a nanny who works with two families simultaneously in one of the family's homes), small or large licensed in home daycares, to large corporate run daycare centers. Since some states have no licensing requirements for nannies, nanny shares, or the person caring for one child other then their own I will not explore these choices specifically, but everything I cover certainly applies to them as well (depending on state licensing requirements in your state).

When I had to find daycare for my then toddler daughter, I mainly looked at large daycares since they were the easiest to find in the days when Craigslist and Yelp were in their infancy. Now there are many other resources for finding care. Large daycares are tempting; many have flashy equipment and outdoor play areas and are less expensive or may have longer hours than smaller in home daycares. But during 18 years of caring for young children and following the latest research and data in brain science and Early Childhood Education, and my experiences working in corporate centers and large daycares led me to work for the last 10 years in my own small in home daycare. As a mother and daycare provider it has been my experience that in nearly every category, small daycares outperform their larger counterparts, and the research also concludes that.

This book will hopefully help families navigate these choices and make the right decision for their child.

Licensed or not, what's the big deal?

Examples in this book are based on what is known in California State Licensing as a "Small Family Daycare Home". This means there are a maximum of 6-8 children (depending on ages) with one adult in a home setting.

Some in-home daycares are licensed for more children with extra adults supervising. Most in-home daycares' licenses have specific limits on the ages as well as number of children allowed and usually the caregivers own children (up to certain ages) are counted in the total number of children being cared for. For example, my original California license allowed me to care for up to six children alone, with a maximum of three children being under age two *or* a maximum of four children if they were all under age two.

All states have different licensing requirements. Some states allow caregivers to care for one non-related child without being licensed while other states allow them to operate without a license if they are open part day and primarily educational (such as a preschool). Some states have strict requirements about outdoor play areas and fencing, and others are less strict.

In California, the home is licensed rather than the person (and in most states there are also educational requirements for caregivers), and if a person with a daycare in their home moves to a different location they must re-license. The reason the home is licensed is because licensing requirements are designed to ensure a safe environment for children. There are rules regarding where medicines, toiletries, and cleaning supplies must be kept, the number and placement of smoke detectors and fire extinguishers, along with what things are or are not allowed in and around the home such as poisonous or prickly plants.

Some states are quite particular about the types of toys and equipment allowed. Fine and gross motor skills are taken into account, and usually toys such as puzzles, balls, and riding toys as well as imaginative play toys such as dolls, kitchens, and/or dress up items are necessary. Some states let you have baby "exersaucers" while others do not. Even the use of swings, bouncy seats, and highchairs are regulated by how long a time period a child is allowed to stay confined without freedom of movement. One licensor told me about a home in which there was no floor play area for the children – "only a row of cribs on one side of the room facing a TV and highchairs along the other side of the room". While she was there (typically a visit by licensing takes 1-2 hours) the children remained in highchairs the entire time. The licensor cited the caregiver for "restriction of children's personal movement".

This is the main reason that I encourage caregivers to be licensed and for parents to find licensed care. I understand that licensing isn't the cure-all to bad caregiving, but at least there is some oversight to remedy such problems when discovered. Also, hopefully licensing helps keep the places that constrain children to a crib or highchair all day to a minimum.

My licensor told me about the crib/highchair-only daycare because I told her a story that happened to one of my daycare families before they came to me. A few years ago I got a call for a tour from a family with a 16-

month-old child. After they toured my home, they called me back for another tour. Sometimes people like to come and see more children playing, so it's not completely uncommon to tour twice. They then called me for a third visit, which is very unusual. At the end of their third visit they said, "We suspect that you may think it's odd that we asked to come back so many times," before they proceeded to tell me what had happened at their last daycare.

One day the father had gone to pick up their child and they found a note on the front door of the caregiver's house. The note said that the kids were next door with a neighbor. The family was very upset and when they spoke to the caregiver she said it wouldn't happen again. What happened instead was that a few weeks later the child's grandmother saw the caregiver and the child at a supermarket. The caregiver had no permission to take the child anywhere (not the neighbors house or the market), and when confronted with the sighting, the caregiver lied and said she hadn't taken the child out of her house. Obviously the grandmother could recognize her own grandchild, and so the parents removed the child. They were understandably very timid about finding another care provider and also reported that many places they had visited used television freely with the young children.

When searching for care, some families visit larger in-home daycares. The last nightmare job that pushed me to have my own daycare was as a director for a large home-based center in Seattle. We provided daycare for eight infants, 16 toddlers, and 10 preschool children with a staff of eight, which I managed. The owner refused to make changes to stay in compliance with licensing codes, refused to give staff an additional five minutes to their state required 10-minute break (it's hard to do much in 10 minutes), and for those and other reasons (such as the owner lying to parents) I eventually quit the job.

Larger daycares are unable to make a profit unless they scrimp on staff. In my previous job, I saw that firsthand, and my response was to fill in for the teachers whenever necessary. This wasn't always possible due to my other duties, and some directors don't feel it is part of their job description. Licensing is very strict about how many adults must be supervising a given number of children. Larger, more corporate daycare centers can afford to have more adults than the minimum required by licensing, or at least a "floater" who can go from room to room to help out with diaper changes and step in during staff breaks and sick days. When you have an adult to toddler ration of 1:8, and you staff that room with only one adult, it is a chaotic environment. Can you imagine having to oversee eight toddlers by yourself? Forget even trying to change all those diapers, give lunch and nap eight children at once in one room. During the best of times there is nothing one can do except control chaos. This is one reason burnout is common amongst care providers, and turnover is high. Children need a healthy bond with an adult caregiver and if staff is constantly changing this affects your child as does being in a chaotic environment every day. Unfortunately, many families need less expensive care (which is what many large daycare centers provide) which better government subsidizing of daycares would remedy.

Although I usually dislike bureaucracy, I believe it is important to find licensed care. It is a good double check to make sure that their home is safe for children and a licensed home care is reassuring due to the licensing requirements of fingerprinting and police and FBI checks for all adults living in the home, along with CPR and child health education requirements for the caregiver. Some employers pay for part or all of their employees' daycare costs. My experience has been that they only pay for licensed caregivers, which is another good reason to look for licensed care. Furthermore, if a child were injured or worse while in care, it wouldn't look very responsible for the caregiver to not be licensed.

What is a small progressive Daycare?

To begin with, it is probably easier to say what a small progressive daycare is not. A small progressive daycare is not an environment that tries to fill every available (licensed) spot with children in order to maximize profits. Nor is it a place that adds more adults as caregivers in order to raise its licensing capacity and add more children. A small progressive daycare is not a place that uses television, computer, phone, or other screen time for the children. It does not confine children to cribs, playpens, baby swings, or highchairs unless only for brief periods of time when prompted by a specific need. It does not confine children indoors either, weather permitting (and there is rarely inappropriate weather, rather, inappropriate clothing). It does not scold, chastise, punish, time-out, or otherwise humiliate and/or threaten children. Never does a small progressive daycare proclaim what a child must do, such as "it's time to play with play-doh!" or, "it's time to read!", realizing that some children may not want or need to participate in those activities at that particular time and that group activities are more suited to the developmental needs of preschoolers and older children.

A small progressive daycare realizes and celebrates that children are individuals to be respected and communicated with, each with a unique personality and with unique wants and needs. It recognizes that infants are different than toddlers who are different than two year olds, and even within these age groupings there is much individuality - developmentally and personally - and that children are always on a continuum of development, behavior, and learning.

More-Kids-Versus-Less-Kids in a nutshell

What large daycares do versus what small daycares do is easiest to see in comparison:

Large (8 kids or more)	**Small (5 kids or less)**
Infants can not screen out noise, so being in a room with many infants and adults is detrimental to their development.	Less kids = less noise and chaos, more calm and relaxed environment.
All children nap at the same time once a day. Naps together limit the amount of sleep that some children need.	Individualized nap times throughout the day. Since they are all napping on their own schedules, each child gets the sleep they need
Kids eat at the same time and are left to feed themselves, or the opposite, which is, they are fed by providers.	Kids eat at the same time and can have help if they need it.
Kids are oblivious to what others are eating due to the chaos.	Kids see each others food and can talk about it.
Diapering one after another whether they need it or not,	Diapering is done on an individual basis, when

sometimes kids will be in a soiled diaper for some time, or disrupted from play for an arbitrary "changing time".	needed. During diaper changes, the caregiver can talk to the child about what is happening, which helps with potty readiness.
Unable to do individual potty readiness, must do as a group even if some children aren't ready.	Usually, children potty train simultaneously because they see their friends and become interested.
Parent communication is brief or non-existent.	Parent communication is daily and can be detailed.
Playtime is highly structured for the benefit of the caregivers. There is little room or time for spontaneity.	Playtime is loose and follows the children's exploration and spontaneity.
Caregiver turnover is high which leads to less secure attachments with kids. Also kids are constantly moved to the next age group which is emotionally difficult for caregivers. Combined with a very low and stagnant wages this makes for a difficult working environment which leads to less than optimal care for the children.	Caregiver is uniquely situated to have control over work hours and income, the they keep children long enough to benefit emotionally from witnessing their developmental changes, they make secure attachments with the children and their families.

2. Nuts & Bolts

Philosophies and Caregiving Styles

I want to touch briefly on a few philosophies of early childhood education and methods of practice that take a different approach and sometimes even push back against the mainstream and are at the core of a progressive interaction with children. All of these practices believe that infants and children are unique individuals that should be given our utmost respect in all matters and situations, including their ability to function on a developmental continuum and to trust that continuum, whereas many traditional practices view the baby and young child as things to be controlled and manipulated or filled up like empty vessels.

Attachment Parenting

The first is a philosophy that is used mainly by parents but is also useful to caregivers. It is known as Attachment Parenting (or AP) and could be described as a style of parenting. Attachment Parenting (a term coined by pediatrician William Sears) is a parenting philosophy based on the principles of developmental psychology. According to attachment theory, the child forms a strong emotional bond with parents/caregivers with lifelong consequences. Sensitive and emotionally available parenting/caregiving helps the child form a secure attachment which fosters a child's socio-emotional development and well-being.

Some of the techniques prescribed in AP include wearing a baby instead of carrying them in a plastic carrier or car seat, co-sleeping, nursing on demand until the child self weans, etc. Obviously not all of these things pertain to the non-parent caregiver, but many AP practices are of value to anyone caring for children and can be adjusted to be applicable.

RIE

RIE is an acronym that stands for Research for Infant Educarers, a philosophy founded by Magda Gerber. Her premise is that a baby is an initiator, self-learner, and explorer, while the caregiver (and parent) should provide encouragement. Some of the practices pertinent to caregivers are speaking respectfully to the infant about what one is doing to them and letting them be an active participant rather than a passive recipient. One quick example that I practice is to wait for a natural break in play or other activity and tell a child that I am going to change their diaper rather than just scooping them up and carrying on. Also, the freedom to explore and interact with other infants and children is a central theme. The practice of broadcasting (which I discuss in another section) is a way to support an infant or child while letting them continue with their own exploration or conflict solving. There is also a tendency in RIE to clearly define limits and expectations, which allows the child to develop self-discipline.

Montessori

Montessori is a philosophy and educational practice developed by Dr. Maria Montessori. The basic premise is that children have natural sensitive periods for learning, and one should provide a prepared environment to accomodate each child's free exploration and natural curiosity for learning. The other crucial part of this practice is the adult who follows the child's lead and does not interfere in the natural exploration and readiness of each child, but rather practices the dictum "pause and watch the child".

In the case of the infant and toddler, the prepared environment would include age appropriate materials that the children are able to choose from at will. These materials are suited to their individual developmental and cognitive abilities in order to be free from dependency on adults for help as much as possible.

All of these philosophies are a means to the same end; allowing young children to develop, grow and explore at their own individual rate and interests, putting them at the focus, instead of a caregiver's abitrary ideas of what might be of interest and importance to them.

Play Based Learning vs. Activities or Curriculum

I recently had a parent of an 18-month old come to me and tell me the family intended to leave to go to a preschool. When I asked why, she said it was time for them to "move on". I asked her what they were moving on to and what preschool took 18 month olds? I felt these were legitimate questions since preschool is a specific environment developmentally designed for children around age 3-6. The parent answered that they wanted more activities for their child and the preschool that they spoke to wasn't really a preschool but a place that advertised activities. I asked the parent if she knew what kind of activities they did with the children and she replied that she didn't. This led to a long conversation about the differences between what I provide, play-based learning, and what other places call activities or curriculum for the young child.

Some Montessori schools allow children as young as 2 1/2, and there is one Waldorf based preschool that I know of that takes some children as young as 2 years 9 months. Early Childhood Educators know that there is a definite emotional, mental and physical shift around age three, and preschools are set up to accommodate those developmental changes. I sometimes do a year of gentle preschool if I have a group that is all close to the same age/developmental level, but in my 10 years (at the time of this writing), this arrangement has only happened with one of my groups of kids.

There are several reasons I choose not to have activities or curriculum for the young child. One of my reasons came from years of watching young children's spontaneous play and also from learning about alternative pedagogies and philosophies. I know that infants and toddlers learn through exploring their environment instead of being led to adult chosen activities. Each child manifests this in different stages, which would not be conducive to random or group activities that an adult comes up with. Also, studies have shown that play-based learning is superior to academic learning for young children because the latter is stressful.

If my group of kids were playing happily, I could decide to engage them in a game with balls simply by announcing, "Let's play with balls!" and throwing some balls to them. They would all participate. However, since they were already engaged in play of their own choosing, one that is born from their curiosity and exploration, then why would my game of balls be superior to what they are doing on their own? It wouldn't be; rather it would interrupt how toddlers make meaning of and learn about their world: by exploration. And that is precisely what having "activities" or "curriculum" for a young child does by interrupting their self-propelled exploration.

Outdoor, Indoor, & Infant Play Environments

Outdoor Play Environment

The first thing families comment on when they tour my daycare is how large my backyard is. I know that it is unusual and I don't expect everyone to have a large area, but I believe that an outdoor environment is perhaps the most important part of a daycare child's experience. At my daycare we spend most of the day outside in the backyard While inside, my front door is always open to my gated front porch, so even while inside the kids have access to an outdoor space. This has been easy to do in the year round warm climate in which I live, but even when I had my daycare in Seattle the children spent a lot of the day outdoors. In a wetter/colder climate having a child accessible area next to the outside access door that can hold shoes and jackets is something to look for in a daycare. Meanwhile, the kids will learn how to put on and take off those items early since they are always excited to go outside and play. You should also ask a potential caregiver how much time they spend outdoors. As a caregiver once told me, there is no inappropriate weather, only inappropriate clothing.

An example of what kinds of things to look for in an indoor or outdoor daycare play area; a child's size kitchen area with with plates, pots and pans, and play food, an easel with chalk and/or painting, pull toys, cars and trucks, large toddler size Legos called Duplos, doll strollers, baby dolls with a cradle, doll blankets and bottles, wood blocks, an assortment of small plastic animals, puzzles, stacking toys, a large basket of hard cover books, a table and chairs for numerous child led activities (or sometimes the kids just like to sit down), a water table with many items for water play, which can be filled daily except in the coldest months.

Some outdoor toys that help with large (gross) and small motor skills should be available such as; toddler sized trikes or other riding toys, a climber with a slide, brooms, a toddler sized wheelbarrow and/or wagon, tree rounds for walking and climbing on, a garden bed or dirt patch for digging and mud play, a few larger outdoor toys like a boat that rocks or a bouncy horse, and lots of balls of various sizes.

One of the keys to a successful outdoor area is to have multiples of the same or similar toys. For example, if a child is using a doll stroller (which has consistently been the favorite toy of all my daycare kids) and another child tries to take it, the caregiver can redirect them to another one nearby. In the sandbox notice if there are multiple buckets and shovels.

Some toys that are inappropriate for a daycare are trikes that are too big for toddlers or fancy electronic toys that do nothing except make a light or sound when a button is pushed. Those toys are fine at home, but at a daycare they provide nothing of value and are basically time and space wasters. Another HUGE no at a daycare is a television and/or computer or tablet. For ages 0-3 these things are not only inappropriate for development but they show that the caregiver is more interested in sedating children than letting them explore their environment which is the developmentally appropriate thing for them to be doing. TV and other screen time should be up to a parent to decide on and control, not a caregiver. Even though the American Academy of Pediatrics has issued warnings against screen use for children children under age two and very limited for ages three to five, I have heard too many anecdotes about TV's in daycares under the premise that only "educational" programs will be shown. Again, screen time should be very limited in this age group and that time should be under parent control.

Indoor Play Environment

One thing I have learned over the years is that children do not need a huge space to play in. If there is a good outdoor space, the indoor space is an extra bonus. The indoor play space at my daycare is my living room that opens to the gated and covered front porch. When the children are "up front" as I call it, they can go in and out freely. The front porch is where we eat on most days unless it is really cold or raining very hard. When we are up front from being in the back yard we are ultimately transitioning (for the children who nap once a day) to lunch and then nap. The children know this and, in fact, after lunch, some of them head for the hallway to the nap rooms without any prompts.

The indoor space does not need to be packed with toys. I have shelves against three of the walls and a couch against the other wall. The shelves have an assortment of toys that rotate every four or so months, depending on if the children have spent a lot of time indoors or not. There are baby dolls with a cradle, doll blankets, and bottles (which I remove with the youngest children since they just take turns sticking them in their mouths instead of the dolls), several baskets of wood blocks, an assortment of small animals, puzzles, stacking toys, baskets of soft indoor balls, a large basket of hard cover books, some indoor riding and rocking toys and a wood train set. I also have a few stuffed toys which usually squeak when squeezed..

As I stated elsewhere, I keep a folding, extendable play yard for separating the room if I have infants. For the infants, I have separate toys that are safe for mouthing and exploring and won't have toddler germs on them. I also keep some toys put away in the odd case of a heavy rain day when we must stay indoors. An expandable tunnel to crawl through and many art supplies are a couple of examples. Art supplies aren't only for rainy days, but I don't leave them out all the time unless the kids are older. I keep the easel ready for painting outside and have a small table with two chairs where they can do marker and pen drawing or watercolor painting when they want to. This is an approach that is inspired by my Montessori background. The idea is to have the paper on the easel, paint and paint brush ready, and a child's apron. The child goes up to paint if they feel like it; no need to announce it's time to paint. The only thing that limits the painting easel from being out is if I have younger kids who would not know what to do except paint the walls and themselves, which is more of an outside activity.

Infant Play Environments

When preparing an outside environment for infants (non-walkers in this case) the main thing for caregivers to be concerned with is safety. A large part of an infants exploring their environment is still through their mouth, so you want to be sure that any area where a caregiver will put an infant down is free of choking hazards including leaves, twigs, and stones. I have a large expandable play yard that has sections to add or take away and I use an indoor-outdoor area rug to create a safe and soft enclosed area on my large cement back patio. This way the infant can see what is going on and explore without being run over by trikes or bonked with balls. I also keep a highchair with a locking strap set up so that if I need to leave the infant to help an older child I don't need to leave them on the ground by themselves. Things happen fast and one can't trust that when they step away from a seemingly safe environment for a helpless infant that nothing will happen. If the infant is up in a highchair out of harms way for a few minutes, that is safer than leaving them on the ground alone. Another option is for a caregiver to wear an ergo or other infant carrier so that they can pick up the infant and slip them in when they have to walk away. When I have had a very young infant in the past I have had a bassinet set up in the backyard out of direct sunlight so the mostly-always-sleeping babe can still be outside with us. Please ask a potential infant caregiver how they handle this sort of situation.

Why are all these toddlers with my infant?

An interesting part of running a daycare is having children of varying ages together. There are some combinations that work very well and some that are less than compatible, but mixing ages will usually be dictated by State licensing rules. In California I am allowed several options. I am currently licensed to care for four children under age two only, or if I have children over age two then I am licensed to only have three under age two with those others over age two. I am allowed other variations with school-age children up to 8 children total, but since I don't care for that age group I will not go into that here. Be sure to check with a potential caregiver about the ages of the current children and how they deal with other ages that they may be licensed for.

My experience has been that having children close to the same age is the best strategy. This isn't always possible though since the prospective families contacting a daycare when they have an opening may dictate what children they end up getting. That being said, popular daycares can keep a waiting list and take deposits to "guarantee" what age children they have coming in. In my experience the majority of people contacting me in my area need infant care. I have considered taking all infants, since my personal maximum is four children anyway, but then I would have to make people leave when their child is age 2 which is a hard sell considering most preschools don't take children until closer to age 3. Ask a caregiver about this if they care for only infants.

A good mix of ages is one in which the bulk of the children are close in age and maybe one other a different age. The best combination is mostly older children with one infant. Caregivers need their hands available for an infant and older toddlers don't need as much assistance with getting around and feeding themselves. If there are more infants and only one toddler there may be some issues since developmentally these ages are pretty far apart. Even having a crawling infant is tricky with a group of toddlers since the baby will want to crawl over and grab anything the others are playing with and toddlers have a hard time remembering to not step on a crawling baby. Again, ask a caregiver how they accommodate for these things.

I do limit infants when I have older children. My policy is to have only one babe-in-arms at once. Once a child is walking I feel that I can handle another infant since my arms are free more of the day. The walking child is usually well on their way to self feeding too, which helps when there is an infant that is bottle fed only.

Taking care of 4 infants isn't difficult, it's just like juggling. When a caregiver knows the routines of the infants – which they learn very quickly – they can predict with some certainty who will need feeding and napping at what times. Also, infants can sleep in the same room, they seem to possess natural earplugs while asleep especially if there is white noise in the room with them, so if another baby wakes up and cries it usually won't wake the others.

The way a caregiver can accommodate infants and toddlers in the same play space is not complicated. One good way is to use extendable play yards that have interlocking sections that one can add to or take away from to increase or decrease the size of the play area. A small infant doesn't need as much room if they are not crawling and as they get more mobile the caregiver can easily expand the size of the play yard. Toddlers are on this earth to explore their environment, which unfortunately includes the infants nearby. Toddlers (and 2 year olds) do not understand or anticipate what will happen when they poke an eye (while excitedly saying "eye!!") or throw a toy to an infant who can't catch or get out of the way. Young children don't have the developmental ability to touch softly every time or the physical control to not fall down on top of or trip over a slowly crawling infant. Also, infants discover the things in their world mainly through their mouths and toddlers are sticking hands and sometimes (even though they don't need to) toys into their mouths as well. This leads to lots of germ spread. Once again the use of expandable play yards are great for these multi-age play spaces, so be sure to ask the question of where/how do the children play inside together to see if the caregiver is able to make a safe indoor play space for multiple ages of children.

I have found that the older kids love to add toys to the infants play area by dropping them over the side (although a caregiver needs to be careful of germ spread when this occurs). Toddlers don't understand that hard-edged toys dropped over the side to share with the infant might not be appropriate for the infant to play with. I always let the toddlers share toys, however, as this is one way that they socialize with the infant and express that they are part of the group. I simply wait and remove the toy stealthily. I don't usually let the toddlers touch any part of the infant's body except an arm or leg since toddlers usually can't regulate the intensity of their touch. This precaution also prevents germ spread. Again, these are things to ask a potential caregiver.

A highchair in the room is handy for unexpected times when a caregiver may need to lift an infant up out of the way and doesn't have enough arms to hold them. When I have infants mixed with my toddlers I keep a separate basket of infant appropriate toys that the toddlers never touch. This way the infant can mouth these toys as much as it needs and their germs won't get passed to the toddlers. If the infant has their own toys, the toddlers' germs from the constant hand to mouth action typical of toddlers won't get passed back to the infant either.

As I have written in another section, playing outside will be different for each particular age group of children being cared for. I usually designate an area outside that can be enclosed with a large extendable play yard when caring for an infant who is not yet walking. I have an indoor-outdoor area rug for comfortable crawling and toys that are of interest to the infant. Again, I keep a highchair handy outside so that if the toddlers require physically close attention and the use of my hands, I can temporarily strap in the infant. Otherwise, I keep around an Ergo or some other type of infant carrier to wear while the infant is outside.

Again, I don't let the older children touch the infants unless it is just on the arm or leg – always cautious about germ spread or too-hard touching. Nevertheless, I always include the older children in what is happening with the infant by perhaps saying, "The baby is tired and needs a nap" if they are crying, to help them understand and feel the baby is a part of the entire group.

Transitioning New Children

When a new child is going to start (unless it is a very young infant), I have the parents bring the child for one or two visits where the parent stays with the child and then they both leave. A few days later, if the family can do it, I have the child come visit just for the morning without the parent. They play in the back and have lunch with us and then the parent arrives to pick them up. Depending on the child's reaction, I do this a few times. This method ensures that the new child has familiarity with the daycare before they are left for a full day.

Children who have been in some type of care before, even if it is with a nanny or relative at home, are the easiest to transition because they are used to their parents leaving. The opposite are the toddlers or infants who have never been left with anyone. For these cases it is a matter of the child bonding to the caregiver, which usually happens more quickly with an infant, but it always eventually happens.

When they first start daycare, toddlers will cry. It is a sad time for them, and even if they reject the caregiver at first they will turn to them for support in short order. Typically, infants will also cry and won't eat much, especially babies that have been strictly breastfed and have not used a bottle before. This only lasts a few days until the infant's hunger trumps their unfamiliarity with their new surroundings. I have only had one infant refuse a bottle from me. In that particular case, her mother shortened her care hours and would come and nurse her.

Toddlers who cry should be given the opportunity to be sad and have their emotions. The caregiver should stay close by while the parent says a firm goodbye and leaves. This sends a message that the parent is fine with leaving the child and that the caregiver is to be trusted. Letting the child cry which sends a powerful statement that we accept their big feelings, and that it is all right for them to have them. Some toddlers will cry and cry and cry, and at some point, the only thing a caregiver can do is distract them to get them to stop. I have only had a handful of children do this, so it won't happen often. When it does happen, I think it's all right to get a child to stop crying if they can't shut off the tears for themselves. Children usually get into a nice routine in the morning with a goodbye (or not!) to parents and then off to play but sometimes months later when everything seems set they will be clingy again. For most children it's a difficult thing to be left by their loved ones even if they are usually fine.

As for napping a new child, I always ask the parents what works at home and try to replicate that (within reason). New children get into the routine of consistent naps fairly quickly. Be sure to ask a potential caregiver how they handle new children and napping.

3. One Day at a Time

Supplies: Diapers, wipes, clothing, shoes, and chemicals

When new families join me I always ask them to bring diapers, wipes, and clothing. I used to let them decide whether to store supplies with me or send supplies daily in a diaper bag, but recently I have had to insist that supplies remain with me. There are pros and cons to both, and your caregiver may have a preference or you can decide what works best for you.

The main advantage to a daily diaper bag is that parents are responsible for refilling supplies. Usually parents are good about refilling, but sometimes they forget which can be a problem if a caregiver doesn't have spare clothing and supplies. The disadvantage of diaper bags is that there must be a place to keep them that is inaccessible to the children but easily accessible to the caregiver. I find that digging through a diaper bag whenever I need something is not the most efficient use of my time, so my families agree to store supplies at my daycare. Another plus to this method is that parents have one less bag to pack every morning.

What to bring is a question parents always ask me. The basics are: diapers (cloth or paper), wipes, and extra clothing. Other items to have them supply are diaper rash ointments, teething relief (non-aspirin) if needed, a plastic bag or two for soiled clothing, and sun block. If you are using cloth diapers you need a wet bag every day for soiled diapers.

Another thing to think about when sending your child to daycare is play-appropriate and potty-readiness appropriate clothing. There are several issues here, and one of them is apparent if you have ever watched an infant try to crawl in tight baby jeans. Infants who are crawling, or even sitting, need loose comfortable clothing to explore their world in. Dresses and skirts are inappropriate for crawlers because their knees get caught in the skirt. Seeing an infant struggling needlessly is a hard thing to watch. Tight jeans are cute as can be but belong on teenagers. Leggings work well because they stretch and don't constrict movement. Children of all ages need clothing they can move freely in, and jeans and tight fitting pants are too constricting for an infant's or toddler's boundless physicality. When children come to me dressed in inappropriate clothes, I change them and remind their parents to dress them in play-appropriate clothes.

Also, children that are becoming potty-ready need pants with elastic waists that they can pull down themselves. When they are first learning to go potty on their own sometimes it is a short time from realizing they need to go, getting over to the potty, and pulling down clothing and underwear. Having a step in between that they can't do themselves is an unnecessary obstacle that can lead to frustration and a wet and defeated child.

Outdoors in the summer I try to remind parents that shorts aren't the best option for kids that are as naturally prone to falling as toddlers and new walkers are. Again, loose lightweight pants are the best to protect knees and also act as a sun block.

The final thing to talk about is footwear. As a parent myself, I know how quickly children grow out of shoes and how expensive it can be to constantly replace them. That said, shoes that are too big are a tripping hazard and need to be avoided. Most of my families get hand-me-downs or shop at second hand stores where it isn't expensive to buy shoes for kids that are going to be wearing them for 3-4 months. It is a huge problem for kids when oversized shoes cause them to trip or are constantly coming off of their feet as they run around.

Food, choking, and the importance of water

One of the biggest issues I deal with consistently is when my parents send foods that pose a choking hazard for their children. I admit that in retrospect I used to send choking hazard foods with my daughter who was in daycare. I didn't know that common things like raisins were a problem or that the size I was cutting her food into were adult bite sized, not toddler bite sized.

My education on what constituted a choking hazard came about through searching the internet for ideas to help a two year old in my care who exhibited unusual eating practices. The child would take half of a sandwich or an entire banana and put the whole thing in their mouth. It scared me because, unlike adults, young children have poor control of the closing of their trachea while swallowing. I almost got involved to help a choking child once in my life, and that was at a grocery store when a mother gave her young toddler crunchy Cheetos. I didn't and still don't want any children choking while in my care, so the best I can do is educate parents on what types of food to send and how to prepare it.

The potential for choking on food is twofold. The most common choking occurs because up to about age four children cannot grind with their molars. To illustrate this, if you have ever seen a small child vomit soon after eating you will notice that complete pieces of food come out. Because of this inability to grind food, there are two rules to follow. The first is that food for young toddlers should not be any firmer than the consistency of a mushy banana. The second is that food should be cut into toddler size pieces, which are about 1/4 of the size of an adult bite. Think of the size of a single piece of Cheerios as a gauge. That is the appropriate bite size for a young toddler. Even 2-3 year olds will stick large pieces of food in their mouths and try to chew it up. Again, they aren't really completely chewing, so all that food goes down their throat whole; thus the choking hazard.

The second choking hazard is when a small, hard piece of food gets inhaled. Again, until about the age of 4, children don't have a good automatic shut off of their trachea (which is approximately the size of a straw) when they are chewing and swallowing, so they can easily inhale small hard pieces of food like crackers, popcorn, or meat. If food items are mushy banana consistency, that in itself will help. I can't tell you how many times I have found hard and crunchy food items in lunch boxes such as crackers, raisins, hamburger, meat, chips, nuts, and a common culprit - uncooked vegetables. These foods are absolutely prohibited and will return home uneaten along with a reminder. Another hazard to watch for is food cut into coin shapes. Think of hot dogs, carrots, cucumbers, and grapes. Cut them lengthwise to eliminate the choking hazard.

One of my food policies that I ask parents to consider before they even tour is the no-juice rule. Over the years, I have found that children who drink juice (no matter how watered down) will refuse water. When considering all the outdoor play we do at my daycare, the kids need to drink water throughout the day to keep hydrated. My daycare kids always drink water and carry their water bottles around with them most of the day. Kids that I have had in the past that brought juice with them would not drink any water.

We all know that toddlers can be picky eaters, however I have noticed that there seems to be a correlation with some picky eating behavior and the types of containers the children's food is served in. I recently cared for two very picky eaters along with two not-so-picky eaters. The non-picky eaters both had their lunches packed in bento-box style containers, that is a single container with sections that had all of their lunch in it. The two picky eaters each had lunch boxes with individual containers with different items in each container. When serving bento-box style the entire container gets plunked down in front of the child and there is no more to eat when they are finished. If they don't like something, they simply ignore that food and eat the rest. The two children with individual containers of different things would frequently look at the container contents when I set it down and say "no" or pick it up and hand it back to me indicating that they didn't want it. If I ignored this, they both would point to their lunch boxes and either say "more" or some kind of other indication that they wanted what was in the lunch box. My reaction used to be to go through offering them each item one at a time. The problem with this is that inevitably I would get through offering all the items and they would turn them all down, meaning that they didn't eat anything. I tried many solutions such as re-offering items, leaving things on the table in front of them and ignoring their refusal to eat, or sometimes just saying "I see you are all done" and taking them out of the chair, which sometimes elicited tears.

One day I had an epiphany and decided to give the container-lunch children all their items at once (trying to mimic the bento-box style). The outcome was miraculous. Neither child turned anything down verbally, nor did they try to hand things back to me. They ate what they wanted and left the rest alone! This makes sense because when we feed children and ourselves at home, rarely do we just serve one thing at a time and then bring out something else. This style of presenting food also mimics how meals are served in most homes, so it also feels more familiar to the child.

Another thing to think about is the size of a child's stomach and how much food is being offered. A child's stomach is roughly the size of their fist. Take a look at how much food you are packing for your child and remember the equation. I have cared for a few children who would continue eating until every bite was gone, even though it was too much for their little stomachs. I had a pediatrician who once cautioned me about toddlers with "no off switch". In my experience this is rare, but it is something to watch for.

Illness

All daycares should have a strong illness policy, mainly for two reasons. The first reason is to keep illness from spreading to other daycare kids or to the caregiver. The second is the reality that kids who are sick usually do not feel up to playing or being anywhere other than the comfort of their own home.

The stronger of the two reasons, however, is the first. I have been tricked by my own second guessing into letting kids stay who didn't seem *that* sick. Also, some parents neglect to share pertinent health information at the drop off time, leaving me to tend for a sick child without a full understanding of their health issue until I have to resort to calling the parent. All this can be avoided with better communication with your caregiver in regard to your child's runny nose, cough or worse.

What has happened to me a few times is a parent letting me know at drop off that they had just given their child a pain reliever (or cough or some other medicine), or the parent telling me that the child had a fever or vomiting within the last 24 hours. What this does besides make a sick child more miserable, is to subject the other kids (and caregiver) to unnecessary contact with sick germs.

This happened to me recently with a bad outcome. A child seemed off one afternoon after nap. I offered the child snack and instead of eating, the child started to cry. This was highly unusual behavior for this child so I quickly got my thermometer out to get a temperature. It was 101 and I called the child's parents for pick up. This happened on a Friday and on

Monday morning I got a text message saying the child wouldn't be in that day. The next morning the father brought the child and said the child wasn't sick. I asked when the last time there was a fever and he said Sunday afternoon and that is why they kept the child home on Monday per my policy (24 hours after the last fever the child is allowed to return to care). By lunchtime Tuesday the child had began to stand around and cry and it was clear they weren't feeling well - again highly unusual for this child - so I called the parents to come pick up. That day my thermometer wouldn't work so I couldn't take a temperature but the child felt warm and was obviously not well. The next day they stayed home and Thursday morning the mother brought the child to me again. When I asked when the last time a fever had been detected she answered, "noon yesterday - oh wait, it was morning". I was suspicious that the parent wasn't being truthful and sure enough, after nap I sent the child home again. In case you lost count, this was three times I had to call the parents to pick up their sick child. The next week when they brought the child back the mother told me that the child had been diagnosed as having pneumonia!

For this reason, I not only stick to my illness policy like glue (see below) but I also do a quick visual check of the child each day when they are dropped off. I will always comment if they seem a bit off, which is usually how I get additional info about medicine given or vomiting the evening before. A standard rule across the daycare world is no return to daycare until 24 hours after the last episode of fever, vomiting, or diarrhea. .

My illness policy is pretty boilerplate:

ILLNESS

Please read this carefully and do NOT bring your child to daycare if they have:

~ ANY cold symptoms beyond a slight runny nose.

~ ANY Vomiting, Diarrhea, Fever - Do not bring them until it has been **24 hours since the last episode** (this includes a fever you may think could be due to teething, or vomiting that you think could be due to eating something that didn't agree with them).

~ ANY rash (except diaper), ringworm, scabies, pinkeye (of any kind), etc.

~ If you need to give your child any medication such as Tylenol or cough medicine (other than teething comfort), do not bring your child.

~ ANY disease such as chicken pox, strep throat, measles, mumps, conjunctivitis (pink eye), scabies, meningitis, impetigo, lice, ringworm, etc. must be reported immediately.

This is a pretty standard illness policy and you should check to see if something like this is in place at a potential daycare.

One thing that comes up the most for me as a caregiver is the question of fevers. According to medical sites, most infants have a naturally higher temperature than the 98.6 degree adult norm. Also, we have all heard (and usually believed, or in my case even repeated) anecdotes about infants having a low-grade fever while teething. I have read that it can happen as a result of gums being swollen. Nevertheless, my experience has been that when a child has a fever their body is fighting some type of illness. Whether they have other symptoms initially or not, I always send kids home when they have any fever at all. Nine times out of ten the children have not come back to daycare until they are done with whatever is going on in their bodies that has caused the fever. Even if we subscribe to the "fever while teething" idea, kids who have fever do not feel well enough to be in daycare, which is the point besides germ spread of keeping your child home if they are sick.

The same thing goes for runny noses. Unless I know the child well enough to know they are prone to runny noses (a specific family comes to mind in which both siblings that I cared for 2 years apart had constant runny noses), I send them home. My experience over the years dictates that a runny nose happens for a reason, the child is getting sick, and most infants and toddlers will wipe their own noses with their hands faster than you can spot the mucous coming out, much less grab a tissue and get to it first. Mucous on the hand leads to the mucous ending up everywhere else very quickly. If the child is functioning normally and playing happily AND I can control the mucous and keep it off of the child and others, then it's fine. If the nose requires 4 or more wipes an hour it gets impossible for me to keep MY hands clean at that rate. Also if the child is "off" a bit, I will call and have them picked up.

After all my kids cycling through with colds several times in a row that they obviously got from each other, I decided to experiment with the "colds aren't us" policy of no runny noses or other cold symptoms. So far, the kids who are staying home seem to be clearing up faster and no other kids are getting sick. We even had a case of the highly contagious (but mild) Hand, Foot and Mouth Disease only infect 3 of 6 children because two children who were incubating HFMD even though no symptoms were present, had stayed home with light colds that were actually the beginning symptoms of HFMD. They stayed home because of my policy instead of coming to daycare per my old policy and only half of my kids got the illness.

Even if your potential daycare doesn't have a strict illness policy I highly suggest you have alternative sick care available for your child. It is a good way for your child to get better faster and not spread their illness to others.

Naps & Sleeping

Eileen Henry, a RIE Associate, once wrote in an article:

> "At 21 months the typical toddler is well past the developmental stage (1.5 years past) of learning the important skill of falling asleep and returning to sleep without parental assistance. Therefore the longer we offer conditions that fix their sleep for them, the longer they come to believe that they NEED these conditions in order to fall asleep. In this case, holding, walking and nursing."

I am not sure I totally agree with Henry's time frame, but I do agree that children will learn the skill of falling asleep by themselves. I have never known a child who didn't go to sleep on their own, usually within a short time of being in my care. It is easier to help them learn this when they are very young, but it can happen with all children. I sometimes hear of parents who swear their children gave up naps between the ages of one and two, but I have never had that experience with any children that I have cared for. It is more probable that the parents gave up on trying to nap the child. I have only ever had one child not nap, and she was two. Also, one of my daughters gave up naps completely at age two but she slept 11 hours each night straight through from an earlier age. All children are different, but they all will fall asleep on their own if they learn how to do it.

When parents tour, they always ask me where the children sleep and what I do to get the children to sleep. If a caregiver has the space, individual rooms seem to work the best, but I have napped children together in the same room successfully. Check to be sure the room is cool since our core body temperature needs to dip for us to fall asleep. If the room feels very warm, ask your caregiver to have the child sleep with lighter clothing.

I always tell parents that even if their child naps well at my house, it doesn't mean it will carry over to their homes. This is exactly why I agree with Henry's idea that we perpetuate our child's difficult sleep habits by not teaching them the skills they need to go to sleep at a young age. We continue to help them go to sleep when they are quite capable of doing it themselves. At my daycare, naptime is an important and consistent part of each child's day. When my kids are toddlers, even the ones who don't want a nap will still walk down the hall on their own to the nap rooms when it's naptime. They know the routine, and they know I will be consistent with naptime, so more times than not they welcome the opportunity to sleep.

I also try to keep the kids in the same nap rooms each time they nap and they each have their own sheets that I change when others use the same pack n' play. The main thing though is for them to learn that nap is a positive thing, and consistency with the routine of nap helps them go to sleep easily. I have always had children who welcome nap – some even telling me they want to sleep - and sometimes these same children are the ones whose parents tell me that they still don't nap well at home.

Potty Readiness

Potty "training" is not as scary as it seems. The best way to start is for families and caregivers to be patient and invest some time early on.

Maria Montessori believed that all children have what she called sensitive periods of learning. What is not always apparent with young children is that the ability to feel the urge to defecate or urinate comes as early as 12 months. It is a bit unusual for a baby this young to successfully become un-diapered, but there are some steps you can take to meet the child's sensitive period when they get there.

One of the challenges of potty readiness is that a young child does not have the capacity to use abstract thought. Similar to a pregnant mom telling their child that there is a baby in mommy's tummy - a child understands baby and tummy, but not the abstract idea – and then when the baby is born the child is shocked and can't understand where the baby came from. So when you talk about the act of "going potty" they may or may not recognize as something to go and do because there is nothing concrete for them to connect with. Taking off a diaper and having a few accidents usually is a good concrete lesson. Although we can't have the kids do that at daycare, it is something you as a parent can try at home. Using sign language during diaper changes is also a good start to adding a concrete to the abstract idea. Children as young as nine months can understand sign language, and a good time to start is during diapering when you sign to them you are changing their diaper or when you see that the child is defecating. It is easy to find signs for "change" and "poop" on the Internet.

Do this consistently and soon they may sign when they need a diaper change.

Have a potty chair ready even if you have a much younger child. Chose a child-friendly potty chair that is easy to clean and easy for a young child to sit on. Put one in your bathroom and encourage your child to sit on it without a diaper when they are in the bathroom (during bath time is a good opportunity). This way they will start to understand that the potty chair has something to do with sitting with no diaper on. Children will then recognize that there is also one in the daycare and will not be as confused or intimidated by it.

Catch them in the act. Many children have a routine or a certain time of day for defecating. If you happen to know what these times are, or if your child has a certain posture when they are defecating, take the child into the bathroom when you see them doing this and sit them on the potty. Chances are they will defecate in the potty chair and make a concrete connection between the feeling of their bowels and the potty chair.

When a child has made the concrete connection of what it means to defecate and urinate, get rid of diapers. Don't bother with fancy (and more expensive) pull-up disposables. Diapers and pull-ups are the same thing. A child cannot feel the difference between the two so the best thing to do is just take them off. If you are lucky enough to have a child ready during the summer, all the better. Once the child has urinated down their legs a time or two they will really make the connection between the abstract word/sign and the concrete feeling and wetness.

Accidents are ok! Accidents are normal and perfectly fine. Don't make a big deal when your child wets themselves. In fact, you can have your child help with the clean up by putting clean clothes on themselves and putting wet clothes in a laundry basket. This leads to an opportunity to practice another important skill; hand washing!

Communication with Your Caregiver

A huge benefit of having a small group of children is that one really gets to know each child and their families. This connection is unique and is one of the best parts of a small daycare. Drop offs and pick ups are seldom a crazy rush of parents running and children screaming. We have our share of tears since losing your loved one for the day is a sad thing, but generally there is time to check in with each family as they arrive and accommodate each child's distinct needs during transition.

One thing that is good to do during drop off is to tell your caregiver about the child's sleep the previous night, or perhaps let them know what time they have had breakfast. I can't tell you how many times I have thought that a child looked unwell at drop off only to be contacting parents later in the day to pick up an ill child. There is something about a caregiver's objective eye that can catch this much easier than a parent. It's not that the caregiver knows your child better than you do, but they see them on a regular basis and it is easy to spot something with a more objective eye.

Part of this has to do with the parent's intention of dropping off their child and getting on with their day. I have only experienced a few occasions where I felt the parent was intentionally bringing me a sick child because the parent had some commitment that they felt they couldn't cancel, but it has happened.

One of the most common tells is for a parent to mention that they gave their child some form of medicine (other than a prescription that you would be signing a consent form for your caregiver to administer) like a pain reliever (Advil, ibuprofen, etc) or cough suppressant before bringing them to daycare. If your child needs such medicine, then they are too ill to be at daycare. It's not anyone's fault that we are taught to treat a symptom rather than deal with the cause. I had a new family once bring me a large bottle of children's ibuprofen to administer in case of fever. When they handed it to me, I explained that I would never be in a situation where I would be administering a fever suppressant because if a child had more than a very low grade fever, I would be calling them to take the child home. The parents were still perplexed so I further explained that a low-grade fever was a good thing because it indicated that the body was fighting the illness and should be left to do its job. Therefore a fever over 100 would indicate that the child couldn't come to daycare.

There is the controversial idea that teething causes fever (along with a myriad of other problems). I used to quote the anecdotes myself, but every child in my care who was sent home with a fever that turned out correctly to be a symptom of illness, I have concluded that the fever associated with teething is a rare thing indeed and stick to my policy. So again, keep your child home if they have had a fever within 24 hours.

End of day pick up is another chance to speak with your caregiver, to find out how your child's day went, and to discuss anything that has come up for the child, the family, or the caregiver. It is a time to celebrate the child's reunion with their loved ones and the ritual of gathering the child's things and getting them ready for pick up (which at my daycare includes a fresh diaper for the ride home). Also, chatting with parents is a lovely way to close the work day.

In The Land of No: Solving Common Toddler Issues

In some states, taking Early Childhood Education courses is not a prerequisite for people opening a daycare. Knowing nothing about the development of young children in one's care can be detrimental to children on a number of levels. The following are some common toddler issues (some very misunderstood) and it is advisable to ask potential care givers what they would do in the following situations.

Abstract vs Concrete, or "If you hit your friends you will make them sad"

Young children do not have the developmental capability of understanding abstract thought. When a parent says, "We are going to leave in five minutes," and is then surprised that the child isn't ready or willing to leave when five minutes has passed, is an example of the child mostly not understanding the abstract concept of time. Another example that I hear about frequently happened to one of my daycare families. The mother was pregnant, and her four-year-old could answer the question, "What's in mommy's tummy?" - a baby. When the baby was born, the four-year-old was brought into the room and shown the baby, looked totally confused and promptly replied, "Send it back!" A child can certainly understand what a baby is if they have been around one and probably form some type of image of a baby inside a large stomach, but the idea that the baby is really in there and developing and will come out is way beyond most young children's ability to understand abstracts.

This is a problem I see happening over and over - just the other day I watched a mother running after a toddler in a parking lot yelling "you might get hit by a car" and I could imagine the child thinking "Cars!! Run!!!". This is important to think about when caring for toddlers and certainly babies. I wholly subscribe to the philosophy of telling babies and toddlers what is going on at all times but to expect them to really understand things that are abstract is setting them (and the caregiver) up for failure.

I had a chat once with another daycare provider who told me about a three-year-old in her care who was constantly throwing rocks when they would go outside. She would tell the child, "We don't throw rocks," to which the child would answer "Rocks!" and throw one. She next tried saying, "If you throw rocks you might hurt someone." over and over again, and was perplexed as to why this didn't have any affect on the child's rock throwing. I suggested she say to the child "We throw balls," and hand the child a ball. This caregiver worked at a large center, and it was difficult to carry balls around while outside given the amount of things going on with a large group of children. In a smaller setting it is very easy to predict a child's behavior if they are doing this, and a caregiver can carry a few small balls when the child is outside or think of another creative solution that will work.

Telling a child that they might hurt someone is an abstract. Telling them to not throw rocks is also an abstract. That is why we always try to give a positive concrete such as, "We throw balls." "Walking feet" is a good term for children who are running in an inappropriate space. Throwing balls and walking with your feet are concrete actions that a young child can easily understand and do.

Sometimes it is difficult to come up with a positive concrete message, especially when there is imminent danger to a child. Sometimes we just end up spurting out the word "No", and this is OK. It's not the best solution, but sometimes it happens, and when it does, you can then give the positive concrete.

Other positive concretes that you can use are "feet on the ground" when a child is climbing something inappropriate and "hands on your tummy" is a good one that will stop a child from grabbing another child or a toy. "We sit in a chair" is good if a child wants to stand in a chair, and "so-and-so is riding on that bike" when another child is trying to get on it too. One "No" that I can never get around is "no crashing" when the kids want to run into each other on their riding toys. I have been saying, "no hitting with the bikes" but if you think of something better, let me know.

Consequences are great for older children, but I have found myself using abstracts such as, "If you throw sand you will be all done (in the sandbox)", but it is an abstract so I try to redirect instead. Speaking of sandboxes, I have found that sand doesn't get thrown far if a child is sitting, so "we sit in the sandbox".

Conflict or No Conflict?

A child is playing with a ball and another child intercepts it and begins to play with it. The first child walks away. Conflict or no conflict?

A child holding a toy yells "mine!" every time a child passes by. The other children ignore this. Conflict or no conflict?

Many times adults will interpret toddler play as conflict when there isn't a conflict such as in the above examples. The only time I step in is if the children are getting physical or it appears that someone will get hurt. If I have a child who has used biting or hitting as communication and things are escalating, I step in. If the children are upset and seem to need some help I will go over and use what is known in RIE as broadcasting. This is a way to help children with their struggle without solving it for them. Especially for pre-verbal children, this technique works very well. Broadcasting is just what it sounds like. Without emotion you would say, "I see so-and-so is trying to take your toy. You look upset. So-and-so is yelling "mine". You are holding the toy. So-and-so is holding the toy." If things escalate, try offering them a different toy. This is the part where I remind you to have multiples of most toys just for this reason.

Taking Turns vs the "S" Word

One thing that I really have a hard time with is when I hear adults telling young children to share. Sharing, when it is used with children in a play setting, is a very authoritarian directive. It is also an abstract. In fact, this is one thing I tell parents when they tour my daycare - we don't share here. Sharing is a concept that isn't understood by children under about age five. When you break it down, you are telling a child they can play with this thing that they really like but at some point you're going to take it from them and give it to another child. One wouldn't tell an adult they needed to share something, yet people tell children this all the time. I like to use the term "taking turns" instead of sharing. In essence it is similar, but the difference is that the child can use the toy for as long as they want and then someone else can use it. In fact, if a child wants to carry the toy around with them all day then they can. That's what I say, "So-and-so is using that toy, and when so-and-so is done you can have a turn". I know it's still an abstract, but saying " So-and-so is using that toy" is broadcasting. It helps the kids feel secure that no one will come and grab a toy from them. Conversely, they don't try as often to grab toys.. The only drawback to this is that sometimes the older kids will look to me to solve a problem, which is when I have to remind myself to broadcast and let them work it out.

Crying a River of Tears

Sometimes we can forget that toddlers are still very young since they can do so many more things than an infant, but crying is still a big part of their expression and communication even if they are very verbal. Crying still happens if they hurt themselves, are hungry, sleepy, or upset that a parent has left. Most of the time acknowledging their feelings is good and letting them cry a bit is fine. Nothing is worse than telling a child "you're fine" or "nothing's wrong" because if that were the case they probably wouldn't be crying. More importantly, you are telling them that their emotions are invalid. How would you feel if you were very upset and some adult tried everything to get you to stop having that emotion? You most likely would not like it. When we react to a child's crying with "you're alright" or some distraction we are showing them that we do not accept their emotion and this is not something that we would do to or accept from another adult.

Some children are prone to crying more than others, especially at drop-off time. After I acknowledge their feelings and let them be sad for a bit, I offer to help those particular children find something to do. This is purely an individual thing, but I have had known toddlers who would stand and cry for 30 minutes if I ignored them, so I try to be there with them and their feelings before suggesting we go play.

The great thing about a small group is getting to know these types of things about each child. Also, when a child becomes more secure and does not cry when they are dropped off, it's a wonderful sign of progress; it shows a developmental step has been taken.

Never Do What You Don't Want Them to Do

I broke this rule recently. I was eating a tamale when I noticed a small chili seed was left in my mouth. Without thinking, I spit it out on the ground (we were eating outside). Without missing a beat, the toddler sitting nearest to me spit out the food that was in their mouth. I couldn't say anything. My bad.

Toddlers are the ultimate copycats. They have the practice down to some kind of science. A few examples of things not to do in front of toddlers (along with my response to myself in parenthesis) are; sitting on a low table (we sit on chairs), throwing a toy into a toy basket (we throw balls), and any other small thing that one wouldn't think twice about that the toddlers will copy. My least favorite recent example happened with my pug. In order to make her go where I want her to I have to walk behind her and sort of shoo her along with my foot near her body. One of the toddlers recently went up to her and kicked her in the side, which I imagine is what shooing her along while walking close behind her looks like. Sorry pug.

Communication with Young Children

I've already discussed things to say to children, but the manner in which caregivers (and parents!) say them is equally important.

Slowly. Toddlers and babies take longer to process language than older children, so give them one thing at a time and say it slowly. Be gentle.

Calmly without emotion or judgment. Children reach a developmental stage near age two when they can be acutely aware of doing something "wrong". Be kind.

Quietly. This goes along with the first two but it is worth repeating. There is no need to raise your voice at a child; an adult is much bigger and can be scary. Be loving.

One other important procedure to remember is my favorite quote by Maria Montessori: "Pause and watch the child". In essence, she meant instead of jumping to conclusions when working with children, wait just a moment and see if they can work things out themselves. The beautiful thing about this practice is that it works more often than not, and you will see a side of children that you may not otherwise give yourself a chance to discover. Ask your potential caregiver if they have ever read Montessori philosophy.

Bullies, biters and bad toddlers

One concern that parents often have is that they feel their child is a victim of "toddler bullying". Of course there is no such thing, but what they are referring to is the child who stands calmly while another child takes a toy from them. This is actually a common occurrence during toddler play. I like to relate to them the story of two children that I cared for at different times in the past. The first child was very gentle and quiet. The child could talk a bit and was the one in this particular group who would inevitably get a toy snatched out of their hands on a regular basis. The child showed absolutely no interest in any sort of retaliation. In fact the child seemed to not care at all, until one day. The child was holding something and another child came over and put their hand on the object to take it. As if in a flash of awakening the child yelled loudly, "MINE!!!" which caused everyone (including the offending child) to stop and look on in amazement. Another child behaved in a similar way but more regularly. Some toys were fine to have snatched away and others clearly weren't – only the child knew which ones. I like to tell parents these stories and let them know that this is one area where usually young children figure things out on their own. If a child has no problem with another child taking a toy from them then neither do I.

The other questions I get from parents occasionally are about "discipline" and "biting".

The only other questions I get from parents occasionally are about discipline and biting. For the biting concern, it's usually from parents who bring me their child who has bitten other children, which they neglect to mention until the child's first day. In the handful of times this has happened, the outcome is that the child never bites in my daycare. It certainly helps me to know ahead of time and I always thank the parents for being upfront with me about their concern. I recently had a parent call me with a child who was regularly biting other children at their daycare. Their caregivers reaction was to text the parents (as if they could do anything about it from a distance) with a message that said "Your child has bitten again". They were very frustrated since it seemed the caregiver didn't know what to do and had no interest in trying anything. Unfortunately, I didn't have an opening for the child or I would have taken them.

What I do if I know a child has bitten before is to stay close to the child and pay attention to their behavior especially when they seem to be getting frustrated or tired. I will interrupt anything that looks like it will lead to biting. I have only had one incident of biting in all my years of care providing and it was a very unusual case and one in which there is a good chance the parents knew that the child had bitten before but they didn't tell me.

When touring parents ask me about my discipline policy, I tell them that I don't have one. Aggressive or inappropriate behavior from a child is always the result of a larger issue. Many times it is the result of some frustration or upset that comes from not being able to communicate efficiently. This is where the caregiver needs to be patient and try to figure out what is going on with the child. The same thing occurs with a biting child. The most common cause of biting is a frustrated child unable to communicate.

As I discussed earlier, sometimes behaviors that we consider unacceptable are a result of the lack of abstract thought capabilities. One child in my care started hitting everything and everybody with anything the child could find that had a handle. Sticks, brooms, and even a plastic frying pan were picked up and used to hit. I mentioned it to the child's mother, and she said she was having the same problem at home with the plastic baseball bat they had bought the child. She had noticed that the child couldn't differentiate between appropriate hitting of a ball with the bat and inappropriate hitting of everything else. I suggested she put the bat and ball away until the child was older. About a week later, the child quit hitting things at daycare and, I imagine, at home also.

Stop a child from hitting or pushing other children and other aggressive behaviors by telling the child firmly, "I won't let you hit your friend." If a caregiver needs to stop them physically, then they should calmly move them from the child being hit or pushed.

The other method I us with a child who is having a difficult time for example, throwing dirt or toys or hitting with sticks, is to have them stay near me for a few minutes. In essence this is like a time out without the child being shamed in a corner of the room. Sometimes children like the time to cool down and when they don't like it, after literally one or two minutes I ask, "Are you ready to play now?". By the end of the one or two minutes, they run off and play and most times do not repeat the offense. Sometimes they need to stay close and be redirected to another activity.

I recently had a woman tell me that she was retiring soon and thought about opening a small daycare to supplement her retirement income. She asked how many children I kept and I told her my ideas about working with a small group. When I explained how chaotic it can be to have 6-8 children by yourself she replied, "especially if you have a bad toddler". Of course I talked to her about her statement, but my point here is that people without any Early Childhood Education training often have old fashioned ideas about children and really shouldn't be running a daycare. Please ask potential caregivers how they intend to handle these types of situations. If we remember that a child's behavior always comes from a source of frustration or other emotion and try to find the cause, there really aren't any tough situations. To quote Janet Lansbury, a wonderful teacher and source of information, "There are no bad toddlers"

4. Last but Not Least

Gender Neutrality or Boys will be boys (or will they?)

The other day I had a grandmother drop off her grandson. It was her first time to my daycare. This particular day, two girls who had arrived before he did were playing as he stood by his grandmother while she and I chatted. This is a child who normally takes a bit of time before running off to play first thing in the mornings. The grandmother commented, "He must be waiting for other boys to play with" to which I answered, "No, all the children at this age play together; they haven't been socialized yet to exhibit gender segregation". I wasn't trying to be a smart aleck; it was a heartfelt response. It is only a product of our hetero-normative society that people believe that boys and girls are inherently different.

In all my years of working with young children, I guarantee that if you dress them all in gender- neutral clothing, cut their hair all the same length and observe them playing together, you would not be able to pick out the boys from the girls. Until they reach an age when society has put its indelible mark upon children's minds as to what is "boy" and what is "girl" behavior, kids are all the same. There are certainly different personalities and tendencies, but they cross fluidly over gendered appearances.

In my daycare the boys and the girls play with gendered toys (for example balls and trucks for boys, and dolls, strollers, and kitchen toys for girls) with equal enthusiasm. In fact, I have to report that the boys are usually more interested in the dolls, strollers, and kitchen toys than the girls are. Perhaps this is because most boys are not given these types of toys to play with as often as girls are, which is a sad commentary on our society. Do we really want our boys to grow up to be negligent parents or unable to cook for themselves or their families? Conversely, do we want girls to grow up unable to use a hammer or throw a ball?

One of my long-term families was a wonderful couple whose child I cared for from age six months to almost three years old. This happened to be a queer couple that taught me much more about gender issues than I had ever learned at any of the sex and gender studies classes I took in my extremely progressive college. It helped that one of the parents was a PhD in Gender and Sexual Studies at a local university.

When this family started with me and we discussed gender neutral language, I proudly told them that when the children start noticing genital differences during diaper changes (sometime around age 3) they inevitably ask, "What's that?" if the child being changed has different genitals then they do. I always reply: "Some people have penises, and some people have vulvas", not wanting to disrespect transgendered people. Although I was told this is a good start, it was pointed out to me that it is not enough.

It is very difficult to veer away from life-long patterns of gendered speech. When I was asked not to refer to the children in gendered terms such as "dude", "guy", "buddy", "man", or "boys and girls", I found it quite challenging. It is a hard thing to stop your mouth from spitting out those traditional terms, yet one should be aware that one of the damaging things about saying them is perpetuating the hierarchical structure that has been inherent in our gendered society. Unfortunately, it is the male gender that is valued more than the female in our highly patriarchal society, which probably explains why in the gendered terms listed above, only one of them pertains to females – other feminine words seem to be reserved for a negative connotation, such as the word for a female dog when applied to a female human.

The other damaging effect of using gendered language is that if a child later decides that they are homosexual or transgender what we have done by constantly reinforcing the society's idea of gender is teach them that what we love about them is how well they behave as the gender that we have chosen for them, not what might be their true gender. Things we commonly say and the way we validate children when they conform to gender norms sends a negative message to individuals who do not naturally conform to those norms. Children need validation, love, and respect based on whom they are as individuals, not based on how well they perform masculine or feminine behaviors.

Another important aspect of gender neutrality is in consideration to the toys in the environment. There is a proliferation of pink "girls" toys on the market. I purposely do not keep toys that are pink (unless it is a traditionally gendered toy like a car or truck). Sadly, the one item I can't seem to find anymore is doll strollers in traditionally masculine colors like purple or blue. To remedy this, I take the seats off the pink strollers and sew a new cover that is a different color.

One last consideration is the way in which we treat the children's play. I have had several children in my care who were "boys" that used to take the baby dolls and put them up under their shirts to nurse them. It never crossed my mind to tell them that "boys don't nurse babies", but I can imagine that may be a response some people may have. The idea that boys can't nurse babies is an abstract one. Young children might not understand the biological implications of being unable to lactate. What is happening really is that the children are caring for and nurturing the baby dolls. Since we really want to encourage all children to be caring, nurturing adults, to tell a male child that they cannot do this seems cruel and arbitrary. Please ask a potential provider what they do to promote gender neutrality.

Anti-Bias, Multicultural Education

One area that I feel is very important to speak about with regards to working with young children (or any age child) is introducing anti-bias, multi-cultural values in their day to day experiences. For caregivers who work with primarily white children, this is especially important. Studies have shown that white parents are hesitant to bring up issues of race and bias with their children. Instead, the parents prefer to have friends of color, avoid acts of discrimination and think that will be enough for their children to observe. Unfortunately, it's not enough. These studies also indicate that societal norms of discrimination towards people of color are abundant throughout our society and these are the messages that children pick up on and internalize from a young age.

One way that young children form their identity is to see cultures that reflect them. This is easy for white children in the West where white culture and bodies are the norm. Everywhere you turn there are white faces and examples to be seen. Less common are books, magazine pictures, cartoon characters, toys, and movies that highlight people of color.

The antidote to this is to surround white children with images, faces and bodies of people of color. This serves to normalize people of color for white children and gives children of color the opportunity to see themselves reflected.

The practical way to do this is to have only dolls and toy figures of color and books that show only people of color. This is easier said than done, but a search online for sources that carry these products is possible. I recently had trouble finding books that didn't primarily have white faces in them (after throwing away all of the ones I had in my daycare) and when I Googled "ethnic board books" I was able to find many that my local bookstores did not carry. The same is true for baby dolls and small figurines. I had to do a search online for African-American and Hispanic dolls and toys.

When I had trouble finding many books that featured more than one person of color with all other white people, I began to change the books physically by taping over the white people with other pictures of people of color. This is also a useful way to re-make books to show non-traditional genders. One book had animals that were dressing up for a party. The boy characters dressed up as a king and a firefighter, so with some white out and a black sharpie I changed the word "king" to "queen" and the firefighters name "Cyril" to "Cyrila".

I am happy to report that even though I kept one baby doll that was white amongst the four others that reflected African American, Hispanic and Asian, the children never chose the white doll again.

Much to my surprise and delight, my African-American daycare kids started pointing to the pictures of Black children in the books and naming them after their family members. Until I witnessed this, I hadn't realized how important this small switch was.

Creating Community

One of the joys of caregiving is seeing my wonderful families become a larger community. The first group of children I cared for mostly came from a group of friends who had been in childbirth classes together. When my first family in Los Angeles found me on Craigslist they immediately called their friends. This is how I got my first two children, and then two more friends' children joined us later. I always considered the families knowing one another to be the reason for the close sense of community that developed amongst the families while they were with me and which continued after their kids outgrew daycare. Although, when a few of those initial families moved on and others came in the phenomenon continued.

Today, many of my families know each other and use each other for resources and play dates. I attribute this to the intimate size of my daycare. In fact, I recently had tea with a mother whose child had gone on to a preschool. I asked her about her experience with other parents at her child's new school compared to her experience at my daycare. She revealed there was no sense of connection whatsoever at the new school. She added that the preschool had even held events and talks which she and her husband attended, but even then they were not able to make a connection with other parents. Since their children spend most of their days together, this is a sad circumstance to find oneself in as a parent.

Here are a few ideas for community building that I have used successfully in the past. The first idea is one that was suggested to me by a couple of my parents. Organize a work party for your daycare where parents volunteer to come help out with the maintenance and organization of the daycare. I was initially against the idea because it seemed like a daunting task to facilitate. Instead, we had a potluck meeting one Saturday afternoon and then during the next two weekends all the families (or at least one parent per child) came over and pitched in tools and time. It was low-maintenance, lots of fun and resulted in improvements to our backyard play area.

Another idea is to offer a reunion picnic. This used to be an annual event, but now we hold a reunion every other year at my house or at a local park. The idea is simple; just pick a location and ask your caregiver to invite past and current families for a potluck picnic. I prefer doing it at a park that has a small children's play area nearby and a grassy space for blankets and food. This low-key gathering connects current and past families and in my experience these friendships last.

A few years ago, my neighborhood started a weekly farmers market. Since many of my families live nearby, I see them at the market frequently. If you have a local farmers market, ask your caregiver to let current families know about it so they can go shopping after picking up their children. I have introduced many past and current families to one another in this way, and they have continued to reach out to each other in various ways.

Some daycares and preschools that I know of also have annual fundraising events such as group yard sales or even a holiday marketplace where parents donate handmade or purchased items and baked goods. These are fun ways to help parents to get together and connect for the good of the children and their families, and to create a lasting community, which to me should be the ultimate goal of a daycare.

What to ask a potential caregiver

Licensed or not, what's the big deal?

> Is the caregiver licensed? Ask to see their license to determine the capacity. You can call department of licensing if they do not have their license posted.
> What other adults will be around the children? Do they have their fingerprints and FBI checks?

Philosophies and Caregiving Styles

> Are they familiar with Montessori philosophy? RIE?
> How do they implement these?

Play Based Learning vs. Activities or Curriculum

> What do the children do all day?
> Are the children allowed to skip circle time or other group activities if they aren't interested?

Outdoor, Indoor, & Infant Play Environments

> Examine the outdoor and indoor areas
> Are the toys and equipment safe and in working order?
> Are there duplicates of toys?
> What toys are available for small and large motor skills?
> Make believe play and art?

    No TV or computers/tablets?
    Is there a separate safe infant area?
    If not, how do they accommodate infants while the older children are playing?

Transitioning new children

    How do they help with transitioning?
    What do they do with a crying child?

Supplies: Diapers, wipes, clothing, shoes, chemicals

    What supplies do they require?

Illness

    What is their illness policy?

Naps and sleeping

    Where do the children sleep?
    How do they help the children to sleep?

Potty Readiness

    Is the potty chair located in an accessible area?
    How do they accommodate potty readiness?

Communication with Your Caregiver

> How do they communicate with parents?
> What would they do in an emergency situation?

In The Land of No: Solving common toddler issues

> Observe them with the children during different times of the day (playtime, meals)
> How are they speaking to and interacting with the children?
> What do they consider a conflict that needs adult intervention?
> How do they handle grabbing of toys?

Bullies, biters and bad toddlers

> How do they handle biting or potentially dangerous behaviors?

Gender Neutrality or Boys will be boys (or will they?)

> How do they accommodate gender neutrality?

Anti-Bias, Multicultural Education

> Do they have POC dolls and books with POC characters?

Creating Community

> What do they offer to help families become acquainted?

Bibliography

American Academy of Pediatrics. Media and Children. https://www.aap.org/en-us/advocacy-and-policy/aap-health-initiatives/pages/media-and-children.aspx

Bigras, N., Lemay, L., Brunson, L. Procedia "Parental Stress and Daycare Attendance" – Social and Behavioral Sciences, 2012. Vol. 55

Bronson, Po and Merryman, Ashley. Nurture Shock: New Thinking About Children. Hatchette Book Group. NY. 2009.

Browne, Naima. Gender Equity In The Early Years. Open University Press. Berkshire England. 2004.

Buell, Martha, Gamel-McCormick, Michael, and St.Clair-Christman, JeanMarie.
"Money matters for early education: the relationships among child care quality, teacher characteristics, and subsidy status". Early Childhood Research & Practice. Fall 2011.

Cannella, Gaile Sloan. Deconstructing Early Childhood Education: Social Justice & Revolution. Peter Lang. NY. 2008.

Chen, Michelle. "How Childcare Actually Causes Poverty in America" July 31, 2015. http://www.thenation.com/article/how-childcare-actually-causes-poverty-in-america/

Derman-Sparks, Louise and Ramsey, Patricia G. What if All The Kids Are White? Anti-Bias Multicultural Education with Young Children and Families. Teachers College Press. NY. 2011.

Gopnik, Alison. What is it like to be a baby? Ted Talk. www.ted.com/talks/alison_gopnik_what_do_babies_think?language=en

Gray, Peter. Free To Learn: Why unleashing the instinct to play will make our children happier, more self-reliant, and better students for life. Basic Books. NY. 2013.

Huntsman, Dr. Leone, "Determinants of quality in child care: a review of the research evidence", Centre for Parenting & Research NSW Dept. of Community Services, 2008, Ashfield, New South Wales. www.community.nsw.gov.au/docswr/_assets/main/documents/research_qualitychildcare.pdf

Kessler, Shirley Swadener, Beth Blue. Reconceptualizing the Early Childhood Curriculum: Beginning The Dialog. Teachers College Press. NY. 1992.

Leavitt, Robin Lynn. Power and Emotion in Infant-Toddler Day Care. SUNY Press. New York. 1994.

Lansbury, Janet. No Bad Kids: Toddler Discipline Without Shame. JLML Press. Los Angeles. 2014.

Owens, Judith . What's the perfect sleep environment for a toddler? http://www.babycenter.com/404_whats-the-perfect-sleep-environment-for-a-toddler_1288072.bc

Riley, Dave, et al. Social & Emotional Development: Connecting science and practice in Early Childhood settings. Redleaf Press. Minnesota. 2008.

Sunderland, Margot. The Science of Parenting: How today's brain research can help you raise happy, emotionally balanced children. DK Publishing. London. 2006.

Tuominen, Mary C. We Are Not Babysitters: Family Childcare Providers Redefine Work and Care. Rutgers University Press. New Jersey. 2003

Whitebrook, Marcy. Turnover begets turnover: an examination of job and occupational instability among child care center staff.

www.researchgate.net/profile/Marcy_Whitebook/publication/22262
3860_Turnover_begets_turnover_an_examination_of_job_and_occu
pational_instability_among_child_care_center_staff/links/55230239
0cf2a2d9e146d5d3.pd

Steinberg, Laurence, Vandell, Deborah Lowe, Bornstein, Marc H.
Development: Infancy Through Adolescence, Wadsworth, Cengage
Learning. Belmont, CA. 2011.

Vanderloo, Leigh M. Screen-viewing in childcare: a systematic review.
London, Canada. 2014.

www.biomedcentral.com/1471-2431/14/205

Made in the USA
Coppell, TX
22 March 2022